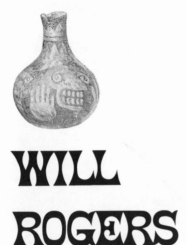

# WILL

# ROGERS

*By C. W. Campbell*

DILLON PRESS, INC.
MINNEAPOLIS, MINNESOTA

8974

Dillon Press, Inc. 500 South Third Street
Minneapolis, Minnesota 55415

Printed in the United States of America


Library of Congress Cataloging in Publication Data


Campbell, Chester W.
    Will Rogers.

    (The Story of an American Indian ; 29)
    SUMMARY: A biography of the Oklahoma cowboy of
Indian descent who became a well-known star of stage and
screen and a noted humorist.
    1. Rogers, Will, 1879-1935—Juvenile literature. 2. Enter-
tainers—United States—Biography—Juvenile literature. 3.
Humorists, American—Biography—Juvenile literature.
[1. Rogers, Will, 1879-1935. 2. Entertainers. 3. Humorists. 4.
Cherokee Indians—Biography. 5. Indians of North America—
Biography] I. Title.
PN2287.R74C3        791'.092'4  [B]  [92]        79-4058
ISBN 0-87518-177-5

## WILL ROGERS

Will Rogers' life was as exciting as the western movies in which he starred. Part Cherokee, he was born in Indian Territory in 1879 in the time we have come to know as the days of the Old West. By the time he was twenty-three, he had been around the world, living by his wits. He worked as a cowboy, circus performer, and vaudeville star. When he began telling jokes in his trick roping act, he learned that people loved his humor. A career in radio and films followed, and his newspaper columns and books were widely read.

A friend to presidents and poor people alike, Rogers was a wise and witty man. "Live your life," he once wrote, "so that whenever you lose, you are ahead." He was, perhaps, the most beloved American in the world at the time of his death in 1935.

# Contents

**I**   THE TRAIL OF TEARS    page 5

**II**   BORN BOWLEGGED    page 17

**III**  SCHOOL DAYS    page 27

**IV**  MOVING ON    page 37

**V**   "THE LIGHTS ARE SHINING"    page 47

**VI**  FROLICS AND FOLLIES    page 57

**VII** "HE KEEPS ON FLYING"    page 67

# CHAPTER I

# The Trail
# of Tears

"Just a cowboy with a lot of luck!" That is how Will Rogers often described himself. But Will Rogers was much more than just a cowboy. At one time or another he was a famous entertainer, world traveler, writer, and after-dinner speaker. He also was the most beloved figure of his time. People all over the world who had never met him thought of him as their friend. Because he had such a keen sense of humor and deep understanding, he was able to bring laughter into their widely different lives.

William Penn Adair Rogers was born on November 4, 1879, in what is now Oklahoma. The ranch was close to Oologah, but Will later claimed nearby Claremore as his hometown because, he said, only an Indian could pronounce Oologah.

Will himself was part Indian. His father, Clem, was one-quarter Cherokee, and Mary, his mother, was three-eighths Cherokee. Although there was the usual American mixture of European nationalities in his family tree, he was more proud of the fact that he was Cherokee. "My ancestors met yours when they landed," he was to say many times. "In fact, they would have showed better judgment if they had not let yours land." While Will said

Will Rogers, "the Cherokee Kid."

*The ranch house in Oklahoma, where Will was born.*

this jokingly, there was a serious truth hidden behind his smile. For Will's Cherokee ancestors had been forced to leave their homeland by the U.S. government in one of the saddest chapters in our history.

To this day no one is really sure where or how the Cherokee Nation began. Old legends say that once, long, long ago, they lived in a beautiful valley in Mexico. By the time Hernando De Soto, a Spanish explorer, met them in 1540, the southern Appalachian mountains were their home. About twenty-five thousand of them were living in a homeland that took in parts of what are now the states of North and South Carolina, Georgia, Alabama, Tennessee, Virginia, and Kentucky. For hundreds of years their way of life had remained unchanged. They would settle in a region, farm there until the soil was worn out, and then move on. The women were farmers who raised corn, beans, and squash. The men were warriors and hunters.

In the years that followed De Soto's visit, more Europeans came. From 1730 on, white hunters, trappers, and traders began moving across the Cherokee lands. Some married Cherokee women and raised families. By the end of the eighteenth century so much intermarriage had occurred that the Cherokee villages were filled with names like Daugherty, Ross, and Schrimsher.

Meanwhile, the whites were turning to the plantation system of farming. Under this system large plots of land were broken to the plow, and slaves were used to work the large fields. The system increased the whites' need for land, and rich landowners became a powerful force in the state and federal governments.

In the village at Tsa-la-gi, built to show people of today how the Cherokees lived long ago, a girl grinds corn with stones in the old way.

Between 1794 and 1819, the United States government forced the Cherokee Nation into twenty-four separate treaties. With each treaty the people gave up a little more of their land. By 1820 their territory had shrunk to an area about the size of the state of Massachusetts. As their lands became more crowded, it became harder and harder to raise enough food and find enough game.

Some Cherokees moved to the Arkansas woodlands where there was room to follow their way of life. They became the first of those who later became known as the Western Cherokees. Others began turning to white ways. Some became business owners and skilled workers like millers and blacksmiths. Others took up new methods of farming and began raising livestock. They built roads, wooden and brick houses, and schools. At first the Cherokees had welcomed runaway slaves to their villages, but as time went on, they began to buy black people as slaves, too. Some Cherokees became landowners of large plantations.

As bits and pieces of their homeland were given up, a remarkable thing happened that opened new doors on old ways. A man named Sequoyah was able to do something that no one had ever done before. He saw the mysterious power of the white people's books. There must be a way, he thought, for the Cherokees to put their thoughts on paper in their own language. He became the only person in history to invent an alphabet.

After the tribal elders approved his alphabet in 1821, it is said that the Cherokees learned how to read and write in a shorter span of time than any other people in the world. Within a year the Cherokees had passed from

*Sequoyah, inventor of the alphabet by which the Cherokees were able to read and write in their own language.*

a state of having no written language at all to a high degree of literacy.

Sequoyah's invention became even more important when Elias Boudinot, another Cherokee, bought a printing press and started the first Indian newspaper. Called the *Cherokee Phoenix* and edited by Boudinot, it began publication in New Echota, Georgia, on February 21, 1828.

By the time the *Phoenix* was in print, the Cherokee people had, in addition to a written language, a constitutional government. The preamble to the constitution, adopted in 1827, read, "We, the Representatives of the people of the Cherokee Nation . . . in order to establish justice . . . promote our common welfare, and secure . . . the blessings of liberty . . . do ordain and establish this Constitution for the government of the Cherokee Nation."

Two years later gold was found in Dahlonega, Georgia.

Eager for gold and land, whites began moving into Cherokee country in large numbers. The state of Georgia passed a law that denied the right of the Cherokee Nation to exist. The law forbade meetings of the Cherokee government and declared its laws null and void. When the United States Supreme Court, headed by Chief Justice John Marshall, upheld the rights of the Cherokee Nation, President Andrew Jackson said, "John Marshall has made his decision, now let him enforce it." It was not enforced. The state of Georgia seized schools and government buildings belonging to the Cherokees. Bands of whites drove Cherokee families off their land and took it over. There was little Cherokee landowners could do since by Georgia law, no Cherokee could speak out against a white person in court.

Seeing what was to come, some two thousand Cherokees pulled up stakes between 1833 and 1836, while they could still take their belongings with them. They made their way west to the lands where other Cherokees had gone years before.

On May 23, 1836, President Jackson signed a treaty that called for the Cherokees to move west of the Mississippi River within two years. The treaty had been approved by only a few Cherokees, who felt that they had no choice but to leave their homeland. Furthermore, it had been drawn up without the knowledge of John Ross, Principal Chief of the Cherokee Nation East. Ross had been in Washington at the time pleading the Cherokee cause with President Jackson and other government officials. Later, when it came time for the Senate to approve the treaty, it was passed by one vote.

In the two years that followed, the Cherokee Nation tried to have the treaty revoked. Many of the people did not get ready to move and took no help from the U.S. government. They did not want to do anything that might show that they supported an unjust treaty. In May 1838, Cherokees were driven from their homes by the thousands and herded into stockades that had been built by the U.S. Army. Many of them died of sickness that spread quickly through the crowded prison camps.

During the summer and fall of 1838, more than seventeen thousand Cherokees began their thousand-mile march to the Indian Territory, in what is now the state of Oklahoma.

The first groups set out from the stockades in the early summer under army guard. They traveled by open flatboats and crowded railroad cars. It was a very hot, dry summer. Water was scarce, and food spoiled quickly. It was hard to take care of those who fell sick on the way. Old people, children, and babies died quickly from exhaustion and disease. Hoping to stop the suffering and death, John Ross asked if he could take charge of the removal of the rest of the Cherokees when the weather was cooler.

Ross used Cherokee funds to buy supplies that would make the people more comfortable, and he organized them into groups of one thousand each. Little was gained by the delay. The rain and cold of the coming winter came quickly, and it was the overland trail that Ross chose which became known as the Trail of Tears.

The children, the old, and the sick traveled in wagons. Others had to walk. Every day they buried ten to twenty people by the side of the trail, John Ross's wife among them. By the time they reached the Mississippi, it was blocked with ice. Fifty years later, survivors still remembered huddling on the cold ground on the river bank as they waited until it was safe to float the wagons across.

A traveler met one of these wagon trains on the trail and reported what he had seen to a newspaper back home. There were close to two thousand people in the train that straggled down the road for three miles. He saw old women, bent forward under the weight of their packs, walking barefoot over frozen mud. He was told that they could make only ten miles a day and that each day, fourteen or fifteen people died. "I turned from the sight," he wrote, "with feelings that language cannot express."

The Trail of Tears, *a painting by the well-known Creek artist, Solomon McCombs. His great-grandparents had followed the trail.*

*Will's father, Clem Vann Rogers, a judge and senator for the*
*Cherokee Nation.*

It is estimated that 2,500 people died during the roundup and in the stockades and that 1,500 more died on their way west. A soldier who later served in the Confederate Army commented, "I fought through the Civil War, and have seen men shot to pieces and slaughtered by the thousands, but the Cherokee removal was the cruelest work I ever knew."

Will Rogers's grandparents had settled in Indian Territory before the Trail of Tears and were spared its terrible suffering. Will's father, known far and wide as "Uncle Clem," was one of the richest and most powerful ranchers in the Cherokee Nation. He had been made a judge for the Cooweescoowee District in 1877 and a senator in the Cherokee Council the year Will was born.

The Cooweescoowee District was far different from the gentle green hills of Georgia. It was a land of high, rolling prairies, wide valleys, and sweet water. Timber grew along the waterways, and wild grapes hung in the trees. There were pecan trees, tall elms, and thickets of wild plum. Deer and wild turkeys roamed the bottom lands where blue stem grass grew as tall as a horse. Out in the open, antelope grazed on buffalo grass so thick a man could pitch his hat in any direction and it would never touch the ground.

# CHAPTER II

# Born
# Bowlegged

The year Will Rogers was born was the year that Thomas Edison invented the electric light bulb. It was also the year that the last of the great cattle drives crossed Indian Territory with thousands of bawling Texas longhorns headed for market.

Many outlaws had come to Indian Territory to escape U.S. laws. They caused so much trouble that the U.S. courts began handling murder cases rather than leaving them to the Indian courts.

"In the old days in the Indian Territory," Will once said, "there were so many United States Marshals and so many whiskey peddlers that they had to wear badges to keep from selling each other. Many train robbers hid out in the territory. Most of us boys knew these outlaws by sight, but that was about all we wanted to know about them."

For Will, the years passed as they did for any boy growing up on a ranch in that part of the country. He spent most of his time outdoors, and very early he learned how to rope and ride. "I was born bowlegged," he explained, "so that I could stick on a horse."

There were plenty of children for Will to play with. He

joined a family of one older brother, Robert, and three sisters—Maud, Sallie, and May. Among his closest friends were the children of Rabb Rogers and his brother Huse. They had taken the Rogers name when they had been slaves belonging to Clem. After the Civil War, the two brothers had settled on land next to the Rogers' ranch.

The old swimming hole on the Verdigris River was a favorite spot for Will and his friends. They would slip off their clothes, take the saddles off their horses, and lead the animals into the water. Then they would grab their horses' tails and float along behind them as they swam. The boys often raced across the big hole to see who had the fastest horse. Will won so often that the others said he coaxed his horse in Cherokee.

They rarely did the things that city children do for fun since there were no towns close by. Claremore was just a tiny cluster of stores twelve miles away. There were few roads worth mentioning, and supplies came to the ranch once a month by wagon.

Since no doctors lived close, neighbors and the hired help on the ranch called on Will's mother, Mary, for help in time of illness. Even before he was old enough to ride a horse, the boy would tag along with her as she sped across the plains in a buggy drawn by a white horse. When Will was four years old, Robert died of typhoid fever, two days before his fifteenth birthday. After Robert's death, Will became even more the center of attention.

It was about this time that the question of what career Will should follow came up. His mother wanted him to be a preacher. His father, however, said little in favor of this. As far as he could see, there was not enough money in preaching. He had a big ranch, Clem said. It would be up to Will to run it when he grew older.

The days did not seem long enough for Will to do the many things on his father's ranch. He especially liked to hunt coyotes and jackrabbits. It was the thrill of the chase rather than the capture that excited him. Killing something on purpose went against his nature, but it was great fun to ride across rolling prairie at breakneck speed after a fast-moving animal.

*Most often, young Will spent his time on horseback, but here he shows off on a bicycle.*

More than anything else, Will liked to rope. He was taught by Dan Walker, a black ranch hand who worked for Clem. Dan was the best roper in Cooweescoowee District. He began by showing Will how to tie the honda, the knot that allows the rope to slip through the noose. Before long, the old cowboy had Will practicing for hours on end. Will claimed that he roped a tree stump in the yard so much that he wore it right down to the ground.

The next step was learning how to snare moving objects. Will tried his hand at anything that moved—from children to turkeys. One day, when he was walking across a pasture with his sister Maud, he had a rare chance. All at once they heard their father yelling at them to run for their lives. They turned to see him riding toward them on horseback and pointing to a bull thundering across the pasture.

Maud ran for safety as fast as she could, but Will was delighted. He stood his ground and waited for the bull to come closer.

"Why didn't you run?" Clem asked as soon as he had lifted his son to the safety of his saddle.

"Didn't need to," Will answered. "I'd have caught him with my rope."

From the time Will was six years old, he heard his parents talk about sending him away to school. At first, this did not worry him since he knew that where to send him would be a problem. There were only a few mission schools maintained by the Cherokee Nation, and they were widely scattered.

Then Clem and Mary heard about a new school at Drumgoole, just three miles away from the home of their daughter, Sallie, and her husband, Tom McSpadden.

Will could live with Sallie and Tom while he went to school at Drumgoole.

Will didn't like the idea of being shut up within the four walls of a schoolhouse. Even the fact that he would be able to ride his horse back and forth to school did little to cheer the boy up. He was happy to stay on the ranch where he and his many friends were free to play and roam. All his pleading fell on deaf ears. It was time, Clem said, for him to get an education.

*The Rogers ranch was in a land of open spaces and freedom for young boys. Will hated to leave it to go to school.*

On the day Will was to leave for the McSpadden home, Clem had a surprise for him. He gave him a new saddle like those the cowboys had, with a high horn to put his rope over and the initials W.P.R. carved in its rich leather sides. Even so, Will rode away from the ranch with a heavy heart.

On Will's first day of school, Sallie put sandwiches, pie, and fruit in a brown leather lunchbox and tied it to his saddle. Tom rode with the gloomy boy until they were in sight of the building. Will went on to the schoolhouse alone. All of the boys and girls standing around the schoolyard turned to stare at him. He tied his horse to the long hitching pole beside the other ponies. Then with a shy grin he walked toward the staring children. Trying to be friendly, Will took his rope in his hand and started twirling it. The others watched him silently. He felt awkward and foolish, and he was glad when the bell rang.

The schoolhouse was a one-room log cabin. The seats were split-log benches that had been smoothed with an ax. The floor was also made of split logs, and splinters lay in wait for bare, unsuspecting toes. The windows were small, and the oak logs of the walls were chinked with mud.

It was a school for Indian and part-Indian children and was supported by taxes paid by the Cherokees. Will, with his blue eyes and sandy brown hair, didn't look very much like a Cherokee. "Most of the pupils were full-blood Indians," he recalled later. "I had just enough white in me to make my honesty questionable."

He liked to hear them tell the stories that his Indian ancestors had passed down through the years. There were stories of the days when the Cherokees were known as

"The Principal People," and tales of Sequoyah, Path-killer, John Ross, and other great Cherokees. At these times Will felt fiercely proud and would often say to no one in particular that he, too, was Cherokee!

Being the youngest of the twenty-five or so students in school didn't help Will to make friends, but he never quit trying to take the edge off his schoolmates' unfriendliness. During recess, he challenged them to horse races. No one could yell quite as loud as Will. He was good in games, too. Because he could run so fast, he liked to play tag and ball. He scooted around so quickly that some of the older boys started calling him "Chiestu," the Cherokee name for the rabbits he loved to chase. By the time the school year ended, they thought of him not only as a true Cherokee, but also as a friend.

After the last day of school, Will gave a whoop of joy, said good-bye to Sallie and Tom, and happily returned to the ranch. For a while he followed his mother around like a shadow. He helped her set out flowers in her garden and rashly promised to do the weeding. Everywhere he went, he carried his beloved rope and practiced on anything he could catch unaware. Even his favorite dog slunk away and hid under the porch.

It was about this time that Will began pestering his father to let him take part in the big roundup. All the ranches in the area took part, and year after year Will had heard the cowboys tell about roping and branding the wild calves on the open prairie. He had roped some of the gentle calves around the ranch, but how much more fun it would be to go after the wild ones! After much pleading, his father finally agreed.

Out on the range it seemed that the boy feared nothing. The more dangerous and exciting it was, the more it gripped him. Clem observed his reckless riding and assigned a cowboy to keep a close eye on his son. Many soon found this assignment to be tougher than anything they had tried before. Prairie dog holes were a constant danger. Will rode so hard that the men feared his speeding horse would hit one of the holes and hurl its young rider into space. Thanks to his skill and his horse's roundup experience, Will returned to the ranch in one piece.

It was the happiest summer in Will's short life, but one of great sadness was to follow. His only brother had died of typhoid fever when Will was four, and in the spring two of his sisters came down with the disease. Will was so sick with the measles that he had to stay in his darkened bedroom for several weeks.

Mary made sure that he had the best of care. She bathed him to reduce his fever, rubbed soothing lotion on his itchy places and made the kinds of food he liked best. She also told him stories to make the days he had to stay in bed pass more quickly.

Mary herself was able to get little rest as she cared for the sick. Each day she grew weaker, paler, and thinner. Then she became ill, and one morning she did not get up at all. Wagons hauled ice from Coffeyville, Kansas, forty miles away, for ice packs to bring down her burning fever. All attempts to save her failed, and on May 28, 1890, Mary Rogers died. Will was too sick to go to her funeral.

It has been said that Will Rogers never got over his mother's death. Later in his life he was to say of her, "They tell that I got my sense of humor from my mother.

*Will's mother, Mary America Schrimsher Rogers.*

I don't remember her humor, but I do remember her love and understanding. If you have an old-fashioned mother whose name is Mary, you don't have to say anything more. Everybody knows already."

Will kept his grief to himself and put all his energy into working on the ranch. Clem wisely allowed him to help with the roundup and with the roping and branding of calves. The boy's roping and riding had improved to the point that at ten years old, he was well qualified as a ranch hand. To the surprise of no one, he wanted to grow up to be a cowboy.

# CHAPTER III

# School Days

Will Rogers had gone to three different schools by the time he was ten years old. Now he kept his fingers crossed, hoping that his father would forget about any more schooling. Will's luck ran out in September 1892. While Clem organized a posse to go after the Dalton Boys, outlaws who had stolen some of his horses, Will found himself at a new school. He turned up at Willie Halsell College in Vinita, Indian Territory.

In spite of its name, Willie Halsell College covered many of the same subjects as the junior high schools of today. It was a tall, grim-looking red brick building. We can be sure that Will would have preferred chasing the Dalton Boys!

When he began school at Halsell, he was awkward and painfully unsure of himself. He found, however, that he had a gift for making people laugh. The laughter hurt at first until he learned to play up to it. As he did so, more and more of his friends expected him to be funny. He had a special way of doing and saying things that opened people's hearts. As it turned out, Will was happier at this school than he had been at any of the others he had attended.

*Willie Halsell College, one of six schools Will attended as a boy.*

Will also made better grades at Halsell than he had before. In January 1893 he made the honor roll. At the end of the following school year he won a gold medal for elocution, or public speaking.

In the summer of 1893, Will saw for the first time what lay beyond Indian Territory. He and his father went to Chicago, where Will sold some cattle he had raised from calves. While they were there, Will went to the World's Fair. He took a ride on the biggest Ferris wheel ever built. It was three hundred feet high and carried 2,160 people. Will rode a camel, too, and sampled foods from all over the world.

The most exciting part of the fair, though, was something closer to Will's heart and home—Buffalo Bill's Wild West Show. Like the Ferris wheel, it was the biggest and best of its kind.

The roping act of the Mexican vaqueros, or cowboys, took Will's breath away. The star of the act was Vincente Oropeza, billed as "The Greatest Roper in the World." Dressed in an embroidered jacket, buckskin trousers with brass buttons, a red sash, and a hat trimmed with gold braid, Oropeza looked far different from the Rogers' ranch hands. He leaped in and out of his whirling loop with the grace of a cat. As a horse raced by him, he snared it by its forelegs. As it galloped across the arena again, he caught it by all four legs. Then his rope neatly circled the saddle horn, and on the horse's last pass, he roped it by its tail. As a closing stunt, he wrote his name, one letter at a time, in the air. This brought Will, cheering, to his feet.

After Will returned home, he worked with his rope for

*The Old Deadwood Stage Coach makes its entrance in Buffalo Bill's Wild West Show at the 1893 World's Fair.*

hours on end. He wanted to make it come to life in his hands. He tried to twirl it so that it would spell out even one letter of his name and tried to dance in and out of its spinning loop. In time, he hoped, he would be as good as Oropeza.

Will put aside the money he had made in Chicago from the sale of his calves. It was the beginning of a nest egg for a ranch of his own. Sometime later he put it to a different use.

Anderson Rogers, one of Rabb's sons, was out hunting when his gun exploded in his hand. Anderson lost an eye and an arm in the accident. Will found his friend lying in a darkened room. When he tried to cheer Anderson up, he was angrily told that there was nothing to live for. Nothing Will said seemed to make any difference. Before he tiptoed from the room, he laid a roll of bills on the dresser. "Here's something to tide you over," Will said softly. "And when you feel better I'll pay your way at any high-class trade school you choose." Then Will stopped in town and with the rest of his savings paid Anderson's drug and doctor bills. Many years later Anderson would say, "No brother could have been better to me than Will Rogers has."

Clem remarried while Will was at Willie Halsell College. In 1895, he bought property in Claremore, helped to organize a bank there, and moved to town. There was no longer much of a future for him in ranching. As farmers settled on once-free grazing land, his holdings had shrunk to a fifth of their former size. Once more, non-Indians were settling on Cherokee land with the help of the U.S. government.

Portions of the land in Indian Territory had been assigned to five Indian nations. Those areas that were unoccupied, known as the Unassigned Lands, were opened to white settlement in 1889. It was good land for farming, and thousands of people sought a new home there. According to homestead law, they could file a claim with the government, live on the land they claimed for two years, and then take it as their own after paying $1.25 an acre.

For the most part, the homesteaders were a hard-working, thrifty lot. They lived in the covered wagons that brought them west until they could build houses for their families and barns for their animals. Soon, tarpaper shacks and sodhouses dotted the prairies of the Unassigned Lands, which were organized into Oklahoma Territory in 1890.

As more and more of the land in Oklahoma Territory was claimed, the settlers turned their attention to Indian Territory, especially the vast area known as the Cherokee Strip. Some of this land had been taken from the Cherokees as a home for other Indians, but more than six million acres were still unoccupied. The Cherokees' cattle roamed freely there, and they collected fees from other ranchers who wanted the use of the land.

In 1893, President Cleveland made a proclamation. It forbade grazing on the land of the Cherokee Strip and ordered all cattle to be removed at once. The Cherokees were forced to sell the land to the government at less than half the price for which they could have sold it to cattle ranchers.

Payment for the land was made in July 1894. Weeks

ahead of time Indian families, in wagons and on horseback, started coming to the small town of Vinita to wait for their money. Others came for the money, too, and hoped to sell the Cherokees cookstoves, pianos, and cheap jewelry by the ton. There were merry-go-rounds, sideshows, and booths selling fried catfish and ice cream. Vinita had turned into a great country fair. Will got $265.70 in payment for the Strip, as did every Cherokee on the tribal rolls.

In November 1896, Will had his eighteenth birthday. He had gone to five different schools, and as far as Clem could see, not one had achieved much success with Will. What his son really needed, Clem decided, was to go to the strictest school he could find for the boy. A military academy, in which students followed rules of conduct like those for soldiers, might be the answer. Will's last school was the Kemper Military Academy in Boonville, Missouri.

When Will showed up at Kemper on January 13, 1897, he cut quite a figure, from his cowboy hat to his pointed-toe boots. Wrapped around the crown of the hat was a horsehair cord that could have hung a horsethief. He wore a flaming red flannel shirt with a fancy vest. His trousers were stuffed into red-topped boots with high heels and jingling spurs. Neatly coiled lariats completed the outfit. It was not long before he was rigged out in the military uniform of a Kemper cadet.

For a time Will seemed to enjoy Kemper. Military discipline and drill were new to him. Besides, he liked his blue gray uniform trimmed with braid and brass buttons. When he went back to the ranch for a visit, he showed off his new finery to the cowboys.

*Will shows off his cadet's uniform at the ranch. The gun is loaded!*

He also showed them how expert he was at marching and rifle drill. With a gun borrowed from one of the ranch hands, he went through the entire manual of arms as he shouted commands. It was supposed to be a display of awesome military precision. Unfortunately things did not go quite right. He struck the ground too hard, and the rifle went off with a roar! The bullet grazed the side of his forehead, leaving a long white scar he wore all the rest of his life. It was neither his first nor his last narrow escape from death.

As the newness of the school wore off, Will became increasingly uneasy. He much preferred the open prairie to the classroom. Several of the boys at Kemper lived on cattle ranches. Will sought them out for some good "cow talk." One of the boys was from a large ranch in the Texas Panhandle. The tales he told of the big outfits there were more than Will could stand. Pretending to have some mysterious but important need, he borrowed ten dollars from each of his sisters and left Kemper. The American frontier was rapidly slipping into the past, and Will wanted to be part of it. He would put school behind him and be a cowboy in Texas.

From the time he entered Drumgoole until he walked out of Kemper more than eleven years later, none of the schools he attended had tried to meet Will's needs or his interests. They required students to run in a fixed groove, and Will was not one to be tied down to routine.

Young Will Rogers's school career might have been far different if he could have gone to a school that had the Future Farmers of America or 4-H programs. School might also have been more important to him if he had been allowed to perform in his own way in assemblies and to study theater arts.

Throughout his life Will pretended that he and education were strangers. This was just part of his show business act. As a matter of fact, he was better educated than most of the people in Indian Territory. He had studied such subjects as algebra, bookkeeping, letter writing, physical geography, and the Bible. During his first term at Kemper he received a grade of 100 in American history, and he was especially good in public speaking. Nevertheless, there were many times in his adult life when Will regretted that he had not taken better advantage of his chance to get a fine education.

CHAPTER IV

# Moving On

The first job Will got after he arrived in Higgins, Texas, was driving a wagon for a grocery store. Soon afterwards he signed up as a ranch hand at the Ewing ranch. When Mr. Ewing wrote to Clem Rogers, telling him that his son was at the ranch, Clem decided not to have the boy sent home. He simply told Ewing to get all the work he could out of Will. Will did work hard, but he didn't stay put for long. He saved every bit of money Ewing paid him until he was able to buy an old gray horse. Then he hit the trail.

Will earned his way back to Oklahoma, driving cattle, but he just passed on through. After selling his horse, he hopped a freight to New Mexico, where he roamed until he was broke. In Pueblo, Colorado, he dug ditches for enough money for food. Late in the fall, he drifted back to New Mexico where he worked on ranches until he was sent to California with a trainload of cattle.

Will's job was that of a cattle handler. Another ranch hand, about the same age as Will, went along to help. The two boys watched the animals, keeping them on their feet so that they would not be stepped on by the other cattle, and fed and watered them.

*At the time Will left school, the coming of the rail-roads was bringing life on the trail to an end.*

Will and his partner had no trouble with their herd, but when they reached San Francisco, Will was worn out. He went straight to bed as soon as they found a hotel, while the other boy went to see the sights of San Francisco. By the time he returned, Will was fast asleep.

When the boys did not come down the next morning, the hotel clerk went to see what was wrong. Will's partner had never seen a gas lamp before. He had blown out the flame without turning off the gas. All night long the boys had slept while gas fumes filled the room. Both of them were unconscious.

At the hospital, doctors worked and worked on the boys but they didn't wake up. It was due to two medical students who refused to give up that Will and his friend came to. The students had stayed with the boys after the doctors had left. Will and his friend woke up late that night. They were alive, but they were very ill. The gas they had breathed still filled their bodies. When Will was sent home, he was just in time for Christmas. Since he was still weak and pale, Clem packed him off to Hot Springs, Arkansas, to rest and let the hot baths steam the gas out of him. Will said that this was the one and only time in his life that he did not want to do any roping.

By the summer of 1899 his illness was a thing of the past. Clem had restocked what was left of the ranch with cattle, and Will was running it. On July 4 he entered his first roping contest and took first place.

Nowadays, steer roping is a main event in rodeos, and often it is a part of a circus performance. It is looked on as a "show trick." But when Will Rogers was young, no one had ever heard of a rodeo. Instead, roping and riding contests were held in small towns all over the West. They were for everyday cowboys who wanted to find out if they were better or worse at their jobs than their neighbors. They competed to see who could ride faster, rope better, and work harder. After Will won on the Fourth of July, he entered contests whenever and wherever he could.

One night he jumped off the train from Kansas City to find a strange young woman sitting at the ticket window. Too shy to ask her for his packages, he left without his banjo. A few days later he met her again at

*Betty Blake, Will's future wife.*

a friend's home in town. "Will lost every trace of shyness,"
the newcomer later wrote, "and I remember my delight
as he sang song after song in imitation of the way he
he heard them on stage in the city." The next time he saw
Betty Blake, she played his banjo while he sang the new
songs from Kansas City. By the time she left for her home
in Arkansas, they were good friends. Will sent Betty her
first love letter, saying that if she would come back, she
could have her pick of the pretty ponies in his herd. If
she didn't take him seriously, he added, "please never say
anything about it and burn this up. I am yours with love."

Betty didn't see much of Will after that, but she talked
about him so much that her friends teased her about her
"Wild West Indian cowboy." After seeing Will at a couple
of fairs, she learned that he had left for Argentina. It

would be two years before they met again, and Will would have gone around the world. Betty kept his letter, though, and later put it in her book, *Will Rogers: His Wife's Story.*

Running his father's ranch and going to roping contests didn't hold Will's interest for long. He had heard that young men could make fortunes in the cattle business in Argentina. He turned the ranch over to his sister and brother-in-law to run, and with three thousand dollars in his pockets, he set off with Dick Parris, another Cherokee lad.

At first, it seemed that there was no way to get to Argentina. When Will and Dick arrived in New Orleans, they found out that no ships were sailing to South America. When they reached New York, they learned that the ship to Buenos Aires had just left and that they would have to wait a year for the next one. The quickest way to get to Argentina was to go to England and sail from there!

And so it was that after two ocean voyages, Will and Dick arrived in Buenos Aires on May 5, 1902. They soon found out that the rumors of fortunes to be had in Argentina were just talk. There was no land for them to claim, and wages were low. Sometimes they found jobs. More often they did not. When they did find work, it was at the rate of seven dollars a month. Dick became gloomy and more and more homesick. Finally, he told Will that he wanted to go back to Indian Territory. Will paid his buddy's passage home and stayed on.

In a matter of days, Will had to check out of his hotel. Unable to speak more than a few words of Spanish and with his money nearly gone, he roamed the streets, looking for work. At night he slept in the city park. No longer did he dream of the big money he had hoped to make. Now his one thought was where his next meal would come from.

One morning, he wandered down to the city's stock pens and stopped to watch some workers trying to round up mules. The mules were not cooperating, and the men were not very skillful with ropes. After he had sat on the fence just so long, Will could not help throwing a loop over the head of one mule. He caught it on the first try. This impressed the boss so much that he offered Will twenty-five cents for each mule he roped. A few days later he was offered a job tending cattle and horses on a ship sailing for Africa. Will didn't care for the work, especially since he suffered from seasickness. Caring for cows in a smelly hold is no cure for a queasy stomach! He set sail for Africa with the thought that things couldn't get much worse. It took thirty-one days of misery to get across. Will was so sick that he was given the night watch with some cows on deck so that his dinner would stay where he put it. By this time Will hated all the horses and cattle in the world.

Once Will got his shaky feet on South African soil, he picked up all sorts of odd jobs. He drove cattle and mules and broke horses for the British Army.

One day, when he was walking down a street in Lady-smith, South Africa, he saw a sign that read, "Texas Jack's Wild West Show." Eager for news from home, he went straight to the show grounds. Will was in luck. Not only was Jack really from Texas, he also wanted to know how good Will was at roping and riding.

Will showed Texas Jack one of his best tricks. Taking out his rope, Will started a slow, wavelike design. Little by little he let out more and more rope until sixty feet of it was spinning and singing around his body. The stunt was called "The Big Crinoline." It was a trick that Will had done many times back home.

Texas Jack quickly offered him a job with the show. Will lost money as soon as he took the job. Unknown to him, Texas Jack had offered fifty pounds in British money to anyone who could do the Big Crinoline. In three years no one had been able to do the trick. Now that Will worked for the show, he could not collect the prize money, either.

*Texas Jack's Wild West Show in South Africa, 1903. A tame zebra adds an African touch.*

Texas Jack's show moved from town to town over South Africa. It was not long before Will found himself riding the bucking horses as well as doing a roping act. Just for fun, he roped wild zebras. Will was billed as "The Cherokee Kid—the Man Who Can Lasso the Tail off a Blowfly." Every time he left the tent he was followed by a crowd of little boys, who begged him to show them how to do roping tricks.

Will stayed with the show for nine months and learned Texas Jack's show business secrets. Then he heard that there was a big circus—The Wirth Brothers Circus— playing in Australia. He was convinced now that being in show business was what he wanted to do. He was also convinced that he could get a job anywhere—anywhere, that is, where there was a circus. Will especially liked the idea of going on to Australia and from there back to the States. That would mean he would have circled the world by the time he got back home again.

By now Will was pretty proud of himself. Not only had he been able to keep from going hungry, but he had also made a name for himself as a performer. People all over South Africa knew and loved him. In Australia he had no trouble getting a job with the circus. Texas Jack had sent a letter with him, saying what a good roper and rider he was. And the Australians really liked his act. A success at the age of twenty-four, Will thought that he was ready for anything. He was grown up. There wasn't anything he couldn't handle.

But Will made one bad mistake.

Even before he left Texas Jack's Wild West Show, the thought of returning to Indian Territory in time for

Christmas had been on his mind. He had saved a little money, and he wore it in a money belt around his waist, underneath his clothes. Will counted his money every day and tried to figure out how much it would take to buy his passage home. He finally decided that if he worked three or four weeks for the circus, he would have enough to get home on.

*Earning his way back home, Will does his roping act in New Zealand, thousands of miles across the Indian Ocean from South Africa.*

Home for Christmas! The more Will thought about it, the better he liked the idea. And what better way to go home than as a top circus performer? Will felt as though he was on top of the world.

Some of the older men around the circus found out about Will's money and asked him to join them in a card game for low stakes. Will had never gambled in his life. It was not a friendly game, and the stakes were high. The men were skilled gamblers. Will lost every cent of the money he had saved.

It was a downhearted young man who went through his roping act the next day. Luckily, Will had never written his sisters or his father about his plans for Christmas. That was to have been a surprise. Now there would be no surprise. Now he must start all over again: After traveling across Australia, the circus journeyed to New Zealand.

All in all, it took Will eight months of work to build up the savings he had lost in the card game, but he finally made it. By the time the New Zealand tour was over, he had enough money to book passage home.

When he arrived in San Francisco in April 1904, Will had been gone from home for more than two years. He had been around the world and had traveled more than fifty thousand miles—most of it seasick!

# CHAPTER V

# "The Lights Are Shining"

"Meet me in Saint Louis, Louis," went a hit song of 1904. "Meet me at the Fair. Don't tell me the lights are shining any place but there."

Will was in Saint Louis for the World's Fair of 1904. He was working in the Cummins Wild West Show, and there was no performer at the fair who worked harder. He was saving money, too. Every penny he could spare was slipped into his money belt. This time, no sharp-eyed gamblers would take it away from him. This time, he was saving for an all-important reason. That reason was Betty Blake.

Strangely enough, Will had not written to Betty in all the time he had been away. In fact, she had not even known where he was. When she came to Saint Louis to go to the fair, she found out that Will was there, too. Curious to see what he was like after two years abroad, Betty wrote Will a note and sent it in care of the show. Will answered at once and asked her to attend the afternoon performance. After seeing the fair and having dinner with her, Will made up his mind that Betty Blake was the one girl for him. And so he began saving his money in the hope that

she would someday be his wife. When the time came for
the show to disband, Will made up his mind for the second
time that summer. There would be no more running home

*Will at the World's Fair of 1904, with Comanche, his roping
pony, which he had shipped from home for his act.*

to the ranch for him. He was going into show business for good. Since there were no other Wild West shows or circus openings, Will decided to try the stage.

Vaudeville was big in 1904. Much like the "variety" TV shows of today, a vaudeville program was a series of short acts. Singers, dancers, comedians, jugglers, and magicians followed one another in quick time. Will hoped there would be room on the stage for a cowboy from Indian Territory with a way with a rope. Thanks to the railroads, vaudeville performers went from city to city all over the country. Traveling was a way of life Will loved, and on the vaudeville circuit, at least, he wouldn't get seasick!

One thing bothered him. Vaudeville audiences seemed to like his act, but they were not really excited about it the way people in Australia and South Africa had been. They were interested in his roping tricks, and they clapped politely. But that was not enough for Will. He wanted to do better than that. One night in Chicago, while he was doing his act, a little spotted dog from a trained animal act ran across the stage. Before he knew what he was doing, Will had thrown his rope at the dog and caught him. People in the audience laughed and laughed as they applauded wildly.

That gave Will an idea. Right after the show, he started working out a trick that later became one of the best in vaudeville. He worked out a way to rope a live horse as it ran across the stage. He bought a little horse that he named "Teddy" after Theodore Roosevelt, then president of the United States. The cow pony was quick to learn, and it was not long before Will set out to get bookings for their act.

So far, Will had not tried to play vaudeville in New York City. In April 1905 he got his chance. Colonel Mulhall was organizing a Wild West show to play in Madison Square Garden and asked Will to be part of it. It was the first show of its kind to play there. When the show ended, Will stayed in New York to try to book his act in the theaters there. At first, agents and stage managers would not believe Will when he told them that he could rope a running horse on a stage. It had never been done before, they said. Finally, after pestering people for weeks, he landed a job at Keith's Union Square Theater during the supper show. This was probably the worst spot on the whole program. Will, however, was grateful for any chance.

At half-past six on June 12, 1905, only a few people were in the audience when Will walked out on the stage. Coils of rope dangled from his hand. He tossed the rope here and there and hopped through a loop or two. Then suddenly, Teddy darted out from the wings with Buck McKee, a longtime friend of Will's, on his back. Will threw two ropes at once—one with each hand. He caught *both* Buck and Teddy at the same time.

The manager of the theater was impressed. He not only kept Will for the rest of the week, but he also asked him to do two more shows every day. After that he played at Hammerstein's Victoria Music Hall, a top-of-the-line theater. To keep Teddy from slipping on the slick wood floors, Will made felt boots for him to wear over his horseshoes. And because Will did no talking, his performance was billed as a "dumb act."

One day a stage manager told Will that because the double-roping act had to be done so quickly, the audience

*Will and his partner, Buck McGee, pose for their vaudeville show stopper. In the act itself, Will snares Buck and his horse with two ropes at once as they gallop across the stage.*

often failed to see the skill required. He said that it would liven up Will's act if he explained ahead of time what he was going to do.

At first Will objected. He thought that nothing he had to say would interest anyone. Just from spending time with him, other entertainers knew better. Will was naturally funny. "What's wrong with giving the audience a chance to laugh?" one of them asked. "Laughter's good for folks."

Will would do almost anything to make people laugh, so he started to talk during his act. Each night his talk was different. He never planned it, but tried to suit the mood of the audience. As it became more important, he began watching the acts that came before his and made remarks about them. In doing so, he looked at his rope rather than the audience. He seemed to be a man talking to himself on stage, and this made anything he said even funnier. When other performers watched his act in the wings, he might rope one of them and drag the surprised and struggling entertainer out on stage.

The gum chewing, which became Will's trademark, was made part of the act by chance. Will was a great baseball fan. Whenever he could get away from the theater, he headed for a ball park to practice with the players. On rainy afternoons, the ball players came to the theater to see him. It was from them that Will picked up the habit of chewing gum. One day he was late for the show and still had the gum in his mouth when he came on stage. The big wad of gum made talk almost impossible. When he heard laughter, Will walked back and stuck the gum on the curtain. The crowd laughed harder.

From then on, Will parked his gum on the curtain or

over the *W* on the card giving his name so that it read "ill Rogers," especially if he missed a rope trick. Giving a shamefaced grin, he would then do the trick over again, collect the gum, and start chewing. This never failed to bring down the house.

Will had begun talking to the audience to show off his roping skill, and roping was still the heart of his act. He began by dancing in and out of the fancy loops he made with one rope. Then he worked up to two and three ropes. He expertly tossed loop after loop over Buck's hands, his head, his body, until he had his partner bound from head to foot.

The Big Crinoline, with which he ended his act, was spectacular on an indoor stage. First he showed the crowd that the rope was almost as long as the theater. Then, mounted on Teddy, he began making a small loop with the rope. Little by little the loop grew larger, and as it did, he lifted the rope over his head. Soon it was whizzing over the heads of the people in the audience. At last the entire 100-foot length of rope was spinning through the theater. At just the right moment Will backed Teddy up and let the rope fall to the floor. Then with a yell he raced Teddy off the stage. It was over, but the audience wanted more. That's the way a vaudeville act should be!

Before long theater managers began coming to Will with offers. His days of trudging from theater to theater, looking for work, were over. Will was in bigtime vaudeville now. By April 1906, less than a year after he had appeared in Madison Square Garden, he was playing the most important theater in Europe—the Winter Garden in Berlin, Germany. Then he went to the Palace, London's

*Will ropes the entire cast of performers in a version of the Big Crinoline.*

leading music hall, for five weeks. While he was in England, King Edward VII saw him perform.

Will may have played before the King of England, but with Betty he was still a little shy. When Will's sister, Maud, invited Betty for a visit, she was caught up in party after party. Will didn't go to many of them, and when he did, he seldom talked with Betty. She was startled when, a week after she had returned home, he asked her to marry him. Will loved life on the road, but Betty thought that it was an unsettled way to begin family life. She put him off, and for Christmas, Will sent her a handkerchief with a note:

> The old Indian lady I bought it from gave me this handkerchief, asking me if I was married. I said "No." She said, "then give it to the wife when you do marry." . . . I will just give it to you as I kinda prize it. And you might do the same.

During the next two years, Will organized a Wild West show of his own that he took to London. With Buck and Teddy he also toured most of the big cities in the United States and Canada. Then, one November day, he came to Betty's home and told her that he had come to marry her right away. This time she agreed. On November 25, 1908, Will Rogers and Betty Blake were married. Twenty-five years later Will wrote, "The day I roped Betty, I did the star performance of my life."

Up and down the land Will and Betty went. A week in this town, then on to the next. With both Buck and Teddy nibbling at their pay envelope, money was a problem. So that they would be sure to save some, they bought a metal box with a slit in the top. Every day they would push a dollar through the slot. In the East it was paper; in the West it was silver. The box grew heavy and rattled like a freight car full of chicken crates. One afternoon in Butte, Montana, they came home to find their things strewn about the room. And there, on the floor, was their strongbox with the lid pried open. The money was gone. "It's all over, Blake," Will said to Betty. "And there's nothing we can do about it except report it to the office downstairs. And since we can't do anything about it, let's not worry about it. Let's go out and have a good lunch."

Will was used to starting over.

# CHAPTER VI

# Frolics
# and Follies

The fact that Will had to start all over again had a lot to do with his staying in show business. Betty and he had decided to settle down in Claremore, Oklahoma, after this tour. Now, with their money gone, they had to keep on touring. Betty came to share Will's love of life on the road. Later, she looked back on the early years of their marriage as their happiest time together.

Will's father had changed his mind, too. No longer did Clem want his son to be a rancher. When he spent a week in Washington, D.C., he went to see all of Will's performances. After the show Clem waited outside to hear what people had to say about Will. If anyone doubted that Will was a real cowboy, Clem would introduce himself and offer a chance to meet Will. Each evening Clem had a small crowd gathered at the stage door, waiting for his son.

Will and Betty named their first baby, who was born October 20, 1911, William Vann Rogers. "William" was for Will himself, of course, and "Vann" was Clem's middle name. The proud grandfather sent little Will a pair of tiny beaded moccasins. The same day they

received the package, Will and Betty learned that Clem
had died in his sleep. It saddened Will to think that
his father had died just when they were really beginning
to understand each other. "All of us children have been
wonderfully fortunate," he had written to his sister earlier,
"in having such a kind and loving father."

Will's career was having its ups and downs. More than
once he had put together a show of his own and had been
less than successful. He had also played in three musicals,
all of which had closed after a few performances. By
1915 there were three children in the Rogers family—
Will, Jr., Mary, and James. Since Will was playing in
New York, Will and Betty saw a chance for them all
to be together. They rented a home in Amityville, Long
Island, and bought a car. One day, while swimming near
their home, Will dived off the wharf while the tide was
out. He landed on his head and was knocked out.
As a result of the accident, his right arm was para-
lyzed. Having no other choice but to go on with his act,
Will began to rope with his left arm.

Then, suddenly, his luck changed. In the next few
years Will Rogers would become the voice of America.
This is how his rise to fame began.

Florenz Ziegfeld was one of the most powerful people
in New York show business. His shows, the *Ziegfield
Follies,* were the biggest and most exciting on Broadway.
Dozens of beautiful women, dressed in jewels, furs, lace,
and satin, glided across a glittering stage. Such stars
as W.C. Fields, Fanny Brice, and Eddie Cantor became
well known in the *Follies.* Was this a place for a
cowboy with a rope?

*Will riding with his children, Will, Jr., Jimmy, and Mary,
near their Long Island home around 1918.*

Gene Buck, one of Ziegfeld's writers, thought it was. He had seen Will perform in a musical, and he saw a chance for Will to become America's first cowboy comedian. But when he told Mr. Ziegfeld about his idea, Ziegfeld was shocked. Ziegfeld could not imagine having a rough-and-ready cowboy in among his beautiful show girls. And yet Buck was largely responsible for the *Follies'* success. Any idea of his, especially one he felt so strongly about, was worth a try.

And so it was that Will, now with the use of both arms, appeared in the *Midnight Frolic.* The *Frolic* was a glorified nightclub act held in the roof garden of the theater where the *Follies* played. It was smaller but just as glamorous.

Will didn't change his act one bit for the fancy show. Dressed in a blue plaid shirt, rumpled chaps, and a squashed-down hat, he ambled out on the stage. Along the back of the stage was a row of gorgeous show girls. Will looked like a baffled ranch hand who had somehow strayed off his range. Before he said a word, people started to giggle. Later, he got the biggest laughs of the show. Gene Buck had been right again, and Ziegfeld kept Will on the payroll.

It didn't take Will long to find out that his jokes were growing stale. People often came to the *Frolic* night after night. These "repeaters" didn't laugh at a joke when they heard it for the third time in a week.

"Why don't you talk about what you read?" Betty asked Will. "Goodness knows! you're always reading the papers!"

Will took her advice and started looking for ways to

*A cowboy makes the Big Time. Will (center) with the glamorous cast of the* Ziegfeld Follies.

poke fun at the day's events. "A joke don't have to be near as funny if it's up to date," Will says in his life story. "Serving only strictly fresh-laid jokes, as you might say, goes better than anything else." He goes on to say that his favorite jokes weren't the ones that got the biggest laughs, because people didn't think about them. "I like the one where, if you are with a friend, and hear it, it makes you think, and you nudge your friend and say; 'He's right about that.' I would rather have you do that than to have you laugh—and then forget the next minute what it was you laughed at."

Every day Will read five or six newspapers, and most of his quips were based on the headlines. After he joined the *Ziegfeld Follies* in 1916, he was doing three different acts a day—two for the *Follies* and one for the *Frolic*. By now his talking had become more important than his roping. People came to see him time and time again because they knew he would never say the same thing twice.

During his act he looked out over the audience to see if there was anyone there he knew. One night, Will heard the cry of a wild turkey ring through the theater. This was surely the first time such a sound had ever been heard on Broadway! Will looked out over the audience and spotted Jim Tally, a man who had once worked on the Rogers ranch. Tally had been taught how to gobble like a turkey by Cherokee Bill, Oklahoma's most famous outlaw. Will had him do the cry again from the stage. This time it was even louder. "Out in Oklahoma where I come from, that's our native language," said Will. "Our papooses learn it before they do Daddy."

It was natural that the president of the United States

would make headlines. It was also natural that Will would have a lot to say about him, most of it funny. One day, when Will was on tour in Baltimore, he learned that the butt of his jokes would be in the audience.

"I had never told Jokes even to a President, much less about one, especially to his face," he says in his life story. "Well, I am not kidding you when I tell you that I was scared to death." It didn't help when a stage-hand told him, "You die in 5 more minutes for kidding your Country." They had to shove Will onto the stage.

"I am kinder nervous here tonight," Will said as he faced President Woodrow Wilson. He was so obviously scared that the crowd broke up. Then Will sneaked up on his president jokes. At first, people didn't dare laugh unless they saw President Wilson laughing, too. As Will tells the story, "He sat there and led that entire audience in laughing at the ones on himself."

Will was still with the *Follies* when, on November 11, 1918, World War I came to an end. Will's quips about the peace conference after the war were quoted so much that he put them in a book. *The Cowboy Philosopher on the Peace Conference* was such a hit that a year later he put out *The Cowboy Philosopher on Prohibition.* These books were just a start on what would be his second career—writing. All in all, he would write six books and countless magazine and newspaper stories.

Meanwhile, Will began a third career. In the spring of 1919 he went to Hollywood with a two-year movie contract. The Rogers family, which now included a new baby named Freddie, moved to a roomy house in Los Angeles. Samuel Goldwyn, the head of Goldwyn Studios,

*Will goes to Hollywood. Here he is on location during the
filming of* Cupid, the Cowpuncher.

had a building on the movie lot made over for their horses. Every day the children went to the studio to ride. Jimmy even got a couple of parts in his father's movies.

"It's the grandest show business I know anything about," Will said about the movies, "and the only place where an actor can act and at the same time sit down in front and clap for himself."

It was during this time that the death came to the family again. The three boys—Will, Jr., Jimmy, and Freddie—were all taken ill. At first the doctors thought it was tonsillitis. As the children grew worse, they knew that it was diphtheria, a deadly disease. Will drove all night to get the antitoxin that could save them. He was too late for Freddie.

Shortly after the baby's death, the family moved into a new house they had bought in Beverly Hills. Now they could have their horses at home. Will added a stable, barns, and a riding rink. There was also a swimming pool and in the basement, a curtained stage where the children could entertain Mom and Dad.

After Will had done fourteen films for Goldwyn, he tried making movies on his own. He put everything they owned into the project, even his life insurance and their savings for the children. He lost it all.

Will went back to the *Follies* and tried other ways of making money, too. He took after-dinner speaking jobs for clubs in New York and went on lecture tours. Just for fun, he began writing for newspapers. Will's first weekly column appeared in the *New York Times* on December 30, 1922. Four years later he was writing a shorter daily column that was carried by more than four

*Wherever he happened to be, Will wrote his daily column. This photo was taken of him in the 1930s.*

hundred newspapers. By 1930 he was also making weekly radio broadcasts. Before long, almost everyone in the nation who owned a radio knew the sound of his voice.

Betty once told Will that he was the most tireless person she knew. "I'll let you in on my secret, Blake," he said. "Most of the folks wear themselves out fretting over things. I never fret. I just let nature take its course and enjoy things as they come."

# CHAPTER VII

# "He Keeps on Flying"

"I am out to see how America is living," Will wrote in a 1925 column. He was off on his first nationwide speaking tour. He went south first and then headed across the Midwest, ending up on the Pacific Coast. This tour was something special for Will, because he could talk to people as long as he wanted to. There was no act to follow his, and no clock ticking off the minutes of a radio broadcast. And when Will had finally talked himself out, his audiences wanted more. "That's the way with an ol' country boy," he told them. "Brag on him and he'll work himself to death." He couldn't get from town to town fast enough. In a tour two years later, he took to the air and hired a pilot and plane to fly him where he wanted to go.

Will was in love with flight. At a time when few airplanes took passengers, he saw that flying would become an important means of travel. He knew Charles Lindbergh who, in 1927, made the first flight from New York to Paris. People made such a fuss over him that Will put them down. He called the things they were saying about Lindbergh "a lot of applesauce." Will praised him instead as "the only man who ever took a ham sandwich to Paris."

A year earlier, Will had sailed over the Atlantic, but once he touched land in England, he did most of his traveling by plane. He flew to Rome to interview Mussolini, the Italian dictator who later led his country into World War II. He flew to Spain to talk with the king and to Berlin to visit the U.S. ambassador. From Berlin he had an exciting ride to Moscow with a daredevil Russian pilot. Stories for the *Saturday Evening Post* and two books, *Letters of a Self-Made Diplomat to his President* and *There's Not a Bathing Suit in Russia,* came out of this trip. As if that weren't enough, Will started a daily newspaper column while in Europe.

When he went to the Republican Convention in 1928, the plane Will was in crash-landed at Las Vegas, but no one was hurt. Later the same day another plane he was in crashed at Cherokee, Wyoming. Again no one was hurt. When he was on his way to Detroit to go to a dinner given by Henry Ford for Thomas Edison, his luck failed him. The plane crashed in Chicago. Will was so dazed, he didn't even know what city he was in. He managed to get to the dinner, but later he found out that two of his ribs had been cracked in the accident. He kept quiet about the accidents for fear it would hurt aviation's progress.

Nothing could keep Will from flying. In his talks and writings he continued to boost aviation. In his lifetime he made more than twenty-five crossings of the United States by air. Will had a special pass that let him travel in air mail planes, even if they didn't carry passengers. It is said that he was the first private citizen to have such a permit. And, according to the records of two national airlines, Will flew more than any other passenger.

No wonder he was given the title "Prime Minister of Aviation."

Will's life was speeding up so much that events began crowding on top of one another. In 1930 he signed a contract for fourteen radio talks for the unheard-of sum of seventy-two thousand dollars. Will gave every bit of the money away to charity.

At that time the country was in the worst depression of its history. Millions had lost their jobs. Many lost their savings and their homes, too. People were going hungry. Men and women begged on street corners and stood in line for free soup. Will was so well known and well loved that he could raise money easily.

In 1931, after their crops failed, many farmers in the South and Midwest had no way to feed their families. Congress debated about how the government should provide food. "What is the matter with our Country anyhow?" Will asked in his column. While those in Congress argued, Will took off to see for himself.

He told his readers what he found. In two counties in Arkansas five thousand families would have gone hungry were it not for the Red Cross feeding them. A small circus was stranded in one town. The people there were feeding the performers and the animals, too. Will said the elephant hadn't seen a peanut since summer. He raised $250,000 in eighteen days for the people of Oklahoma, Texas, and Arkansas. He asked that it be divided evenly among those living on farms and in cities and that part of it be set aside to help Cherokees in need.

"I love you, Will Rogers, and I don't care who knows it," Helen Keller told him. Blind and deaf herself, Keller was a great leader and helper of the handicapped. Will gave generously to her cause. She saw through her fingers, and she told Will that her fingers could find the humor in his face.

On tour Will gave programs in hospitals and jails. He visited crippled children and disabled soldiers. After leaving them laughing, he might be found in some hidden spot, sobbing like a broken-hearted child. He gave his time and his money to people not just because they needed it, but because he cared for them.

Will had a lot to say about politics and world affairs. Now people across the country felt as if they knew him and his opinions very well. They heard his voice on radio, and they read his newspaper columns every day. The people in Oklahoma were really proud of Will. There was talk that he should run for president, but Will would have nothing to do with the idea. "Gosh, if people ever begin to take me seriously, I'm sunk," he said.

Nevertheless, some people from home refused to give up their dream. On the first ballot at the 1932 Democratic Convention, he was nominated for president. All of Oklahoma's twenty-two votes were cast in his favor. Franklin D. Roosevelt won the nomination, but for the rest of his life, Will Rogers was to be the "unofficial" president of the United States.

Will had the same luck in movies that he had had in vaudeville. He wasn't at his best in "dumb shows," either behind the footlights or in front of the camera. You had to listen to Will to love him. It was not until movies with sound came in that Will became a big film star. He signed a contract with Twentieth Century-

*Will, all dressed up for his first "talkie,"* They Had to See Paris.

Fox to do talking pictures. In his first picture, *They Had to See Paris,* Will played a millionaire from Oklahoma who took his family to Paris. Its success meant a lot to Will, who wanted to spend more time at home. "If I am a success, I won't have to go around the country and speak to everybody in person. Instead, I can send it to them in a [film] can. I can spend more time with my family."

Will also wanted the children of America to get to know him as their parents had. When he was on tour, he noticed that there were many more older people in the audience than young ones. The children would rather go to the movies! Will's "talkies" came to be so successful that in many towns and cities school was let out so that school-children could see Will's movies in the afternoon. And, in a poll taken of theater owners in 1934, he led all male stars at the box office.

Will's children were growing up. This made him feel a bit sad whenever he thought about it. Will, Jr., was going to Stanford University; Mary, to Sarah Lawrence College; and Jim, to Webb College. Later, the Rogers children proved to be as independent as their father. Will, Jr., who wanted to be a newspaper reporter, said that he would never try to make money on his famous name. Jim turned down several business offers of his father's to become a rancher. Mary, who loved acting, was to work in a movie and several plays as Mary Howard before she was recognized as Will's daughter.

Since 1928 the family had been living on a big ranch in Santa Monica. When Will was home, he often spent time after dinner roping calves in the corral. Huge floodlights made it possible for this sort of fun to go on after dark,

*The Rogers family at home on the ranch. Will, Jr., is on the left. Jimmy holds Sarah, their pet calf, and Betty, Mary, and Will are seated on the couch with their dog, Jock.*

and Will's neighbors often joined him. After the same calves had been roped a number of times, they grew too tame to cooperate. Then Will sent them to another ranch in trade for some wild ones. If the weather was bad, Will just moved his roping inside, where he had a stuffed calf rigged out with rollers on its feet. The calf was wheeled out into the high-ceilinged living room, where Will and the boys practiced.

Will was in his fifties, but he was as restless as ever. Betty never knew where he would go and what he would do next. When he finished his last movie, *Steamboat Round the Bend,* he flew to Mexico to relax with Wiley Post, a friend from Oklahoma.

Post had flown around the world twice, the second time by himself. Will had been a great admirer of his for a long time. Wiley, said Will, was just about the greatest flier in the world. Post had been to Alaska and wanted to go back and see if it would be possible to set up an air route for mail and passengers between Alaska and Russia. If so, planes could avoid a much longer flight over the Pacific.

On the flight back to California, Wiley asked Will if he would like to go along. Will said he'd think about it if Wiley promised him a chance to find out if reindeer were as hard to rope as steers. Will said he also wanted a dogsled ride to see what "Arctic hayburners" could do. Wiley agreed to the terms.

On August 3, 1935, Will, his pockets stuffed with rolled-up newspapers, took the night plane to San Fransisco. Then he went on to Seattle, where he met Wiley.

Soon the two were in Juneau, Alaska. Will was in high spirits. He was really looking forward to seeing a new country and making new friends. When they reached

*Children in Fairbanks, Alaska, say goodbye to Will (on wing) and Wiley before they take off on their last flight, August 15, 1935.*

Anchorage, Will sent a wire to Mary. It said, "Wish you were along. How is your acting? You and Mama wire me all the news to Nome. Going to Point Barrow today. Furthest point of land on the whole American continent. Lots of love. Don't worry."

Will and Wiley didn't reach Point Barrow. Lost in heavy fog, they landed fifteen miles away. Clare Okpeaha, an Eskimo who saw them touch down, gave them directions to the little town. The plane took off, and then the engine sputtered. Okpeaha saw it go into a turn, nose dive into the water, and turn over, end over end. He called to Will and Wiley, but no answer came from the wrecked plane.

Okpeaha walked the miles to the village, and from there the news went out: "Point Barrow—Alaska. Will Rogers, America's homespun king of humorists, and Wiley Post, globe circling ace of the air, crashed to death on the bank of a shallow stream near this Arctic frontier town last night." Will Rogers and Wiley Post had died on August 15, 1935. At the crash site, the people who were taking the bodies back heard the chanting of songs for the dead. Eskimo and Cherokee had met.

The nation went into shock. People found it hard to believe that death, which had threatened Will more than once, had reached through the Arctic fog and taken their friend. Almost all other news was pushed from the front pages of the newspapers. Messages came from President Roosevelt, former President Hoover, top leaders in the House and Senate, and members of the Cabinet. One came from the Prince of Wales, heir to the throne of England, who had played polo with Will. Still others came from France, Italy, Japan, and other

*Statue of Will Rogers at the Will Rogers Memorial in Clare-more, Oklahoma. At its base is one of Will's sayings—"I never met a man I didn't like." It is a copy of the statue that stands in Statuary Hall, Washington, D.C., where famous Americans from each state are honored.*

countries around the world. Six thousand hoboes went into official mourning for a month.

On the day of Will's funeral, the governor of California gave an order. At two o'clock there was a moment of silence all over the state. Flags flew at half mast over government buildings. Across the country, in New York City, planes flew high overhead, trailing black banners in Will's memory. Author Irvin Cobb, a longtime friend of Will's, wrote, "There was a funeral here today for Will Rogers, but they can't bury that man. Will, he keeps on flying."

Will had some thoughts of his own on living and dying. When Will Durant, a great scholar and thinker, asked him to write something for Durant's book, *Living Philosophies,* Will had this to say.

> We are just here for a spell and pass on . . . Believe in something for another World, but don't be too set on what it is, and you won't start out that life with a disappointment. Live your life so that whenever you lose, you are ahead.

## THE AUTHOR

C.W. Campbell was born and raised in the picturesque Shenandoah Valley of Virginia. Since 1967, he has lived in Great Falls, Montana. His enduring interest in the heritage of the United States is reflected in his articles on word origins and history, and his short stories. Mr. Campbell's articles and stories have appeared in many leading magazines, as well as literary and religious publications. He is the author of *Sequoyah, The Story of an American Indian,* also published by Dillon Press.

*Photographs reproduced through the courtesy of the Academy of Motion Picture Arts and Sciences, the Cherokee National Historical Society, the Film Stills Archive of the Museum of Modern Art, Nebraska State Historical Society, the Will Rogers Memorial, the Western History Collection of the University of Oklahoma Library, and the Woolaroc Museum.*

OTHER BIOGRAPHIES
IN THIS SERIES ARE

William Beltz
Robert Bennett
Black Hawk
Crazy Horse
Geronimo
Oscar Howe
Ishi
Pauline Johnson
Chief Joseph
Maria Martinez
George Morrison
Daisy Hooee Nampeyo
Michael Naranjo
Osceola
Powhatan
Red Cloud
John Ross
Sacagawea
Sealth
Sequoyah
Sitting Bull
Maria Tallchief
Tecumseh
Jim Thorpe
Tomo-chi-chi
Little Turtle
Pablita Velarde
William Warren
Alford Waters
Annie Wauneka
Sarah Winnemucca
Wovoka